Crabs

By Sally Cowan

There are lots of crabs!

Crabs can be little,
and crabs can be big.

This crab is little.

Crabs have shells
and ten legs.

They have two big legs that
can nip and crush things.

shell

legs

This mud crab is big.

When a crab gets too big,
its shell cracks and falls off!

thick shell

thin shell

Big fish and gulls can snack on crabs.

But crabs can cram into thin cracks in the rocks.

Big fish can not get them.

Gulls can get crabs.

But crabs are quick.

They can dig in the sand and get away.

We can snack on crabs, too!

They are yum.

Crack!

It's fun to look at crabs
as they criss-cross the sand.

But do not pick crabs up!

They can nip.

CHECKING FOR MEANING

1. How many legs does a crab have? *(Literal)*

2. What do crabs do with their two big legs? *(Literal)*

3. Why does a crab's shell crack before it falls off? *(Inferential)*

EXTENDING VOCABULARY

crush	What do things look like when they have been crushed? What would crabs crush?
cram	What is the meaning of *cram*? What are other words that have a similar meaning and could have been used instead? E.g. squash, squeeze.
criss-cross	Can you draw a pattern with your finger that shows how a crab moves when it criss-crosses? What is another way of describing how they move? E.g. zig-zag.

MOVING BEYOND THE TEXT

1. Talk about different ways crabs protect themselves.

2. Have you ever eaten crab? What did it taste like? Did you enjoy it?

3. What other sea creatures do you know of that have a shell?

4. Find out more about the way crabs move. Which direction do they go when they criss-cross?

SPEED SOUNDS

bl	gl	cr	fr	st

PRACTICE WORDS

crab

crabs

crush

cram

cracks

criss-
cross